On Teaching Literature

On Teaching Literature

NORTHROP FRYE

HARCOURT BRACE JOVANOVICH, INC.

New York Chicago San Francisco Atlanta Dallas

NORTHROP FRYE was born in Sherbrooke, Quebec, Canada, on July 14, 1912. He is a graduate of the University of Toronto and of Merton College, Oxford, and is University Professor at the University of Toronto. He has remained at Toronto throughout his career, though he has taught full terms at Harvard, Princeton, Berkeley, Oxford, and elsewhere. He has received many honorary degrees from universities in the United States and Canada, and many medals, prizes, and awards in Canada for distinguished contributions to Canadian culture and education. He was one of the founding members of the Ontario Curriculum Institute, whose reports were edited by him with an introduction under the title *Design for Learning* (1962). Of his fourteen books, perhaps the most important for educators are *Anatomy of Criticism* (1957); *The Well-Tempered Critic* (1963); *The Educated Imagination* (1963); *The Modern Century* (1967); and *The Critical Path* (1971).

Hardbound ISBN: 0-15-333499-1

Paperbound ISBN: 0-15-333498-3

Library of Congress Catalog Card Number: 72-84815

PRINTED IN THE UNITED STATES OF AMERICA

On Teaching Literature

IN THIS ESSAY I am trying to set down some of my views about literature as a subject of teaching and learning. The occasion for the essay is the appearance of the first of a set of books under the running title of *Literature: Uses of the Imagination.* These books, with their successors, have some relation to those views. Hence they are frequently referred to, especially for examples.

1

The Hidden Likenesses of Literature: A Search for Theory

IN EVERY SUBJECT that can be taught there are certain rudiments to be learned first, and whatever is learned afterward has to have some kind of connection with those rudiments. For example, if we are teaching music, we can begin with the octave, the twelve semitones of the octave that make up the chromatic scale, the relation of the major and minor modes to that scale, and the way in which such musical elements are presented in notation. Knowing these rudiments will not enable us to compose like Beethoven, but it is a start in putting ourselves in command of the same technical apparatus that Beethoven worked with all his life. Such teaching is progressive in a way that "music appreciation" by itself is not. For many reasons teachers have been for a long time confused about how to teach literature (*and* language, but that is another subject) systematically and progressively, and hence their students often grow up with, at best, only a vague memory of attempts to get them to "appreciate" "good literature." The present series of books is designed to help a teacher to present literature in the same kind of coherent and planned sequence that one might use to present music or mathematics. The principles on which these books are based are the subject of what follows.

In learning some subjects we are forced to depend a good deal on sheer memorization. Political geography is one such subject. There is no reason why Bolivia should be in South America instead of Africa: it just is, and we have to remember the fact. If we try to teach literature without any principles of its construction in our minds, we are going to force a great deal of memorization on our students: names and dates of writers, historical and cultural facts associated with literature, allusions and references and other aspects of content, and so on. One great advantage of teaching literature systematically is that it then turns out to be a structure, like mathematics or science, and the memory work involved becomes a good deal simpler when there is something to hook it on to.

The first principle of literary structure is that all literary works are so presented that they move in time, like music, and yet, because they are structures, they can also be studied all in one piece, like paintings. First of all, we must read, or listen to someone read, or listen to a play in a theater. This is a participating act: we *follow* the structure as it unfolds in time. It is also a precritical act: we are not studying or judging or commenting at this stage, but suspending all mental operations until the end to get a sense of the total form. Study and criticism begin at the second stage, where we see the structure frozen into a simultaneous pattern. For this second stage we have to have a printed text; but study of the printed text does not replace the original listening experience. In practice we may read or study dramas that we have not seen in the theater, but even so we should keep some kind of ideal performance of them in our minds. And even if we are just reading for relaxation, not concerned with an educational process and so not going on to the second stage of study and analysis, we can still be aware that our reading experiences are attaching themselves to one another, and forming a larger pattern.

The word *convention* expresses one very important kind of similarity that we find in our reading. A detective story is a simple example of a conventional form: we know before we start reading it that there is going to be a corpse, a number of suspects, police called in, an inquest, and the eventual discovery of the murderer just at the end. If we bought a detective story and didn't find this kind of material in it we'd feel cheated. Of course every individual work of literature has to be just enough different from all the others to make reading it a distinct experience. But the similarities within the type are equally important. A radio or television serial will use the same characters, the same incidents, the same turns of speech, and if these familiar features didn't turn up, that program's ratings would go down fast and far. So there are aspects of literary experience that are very like games. Each game of chess or bridge may be different, but the conditions within which the game is played do not change. We notice too that it is in popular forms like the detective story where this rules-of-a-game feeling is strongest. The word *genre,* like the word *convention,* expresses a similar sense of classification or type in the things we read. If we are told in advance that what we are going to read is a comedy or tragedy or romance or novel, we expect certain features that we should not expect if the indication were different.

A work of literature, therefore, not only has a narrative movement and a unified structure: it also has a context within literature, and it will be more like certain works of literature than like others. The first step in teaching literature systematically, then, is to establish a context within literature for each work being studied, first for the teacher, and eventually for the student as well.

Detective stories and the like are commercial products of a specific society, designed to meet a specific social demand, so it is perhaps not so surprising to find similarities among them. But when we turn to the popular literature of "primitive" (i.e., technologically less-developed) societies, and study their folk tales and myths, we find the same kind of similarities turning up. Sometimes, where the similarities are very striking and the societies that tell these stories are very far apart, we may even find the likenesses uncanny, and feel impelled to invent historical theories about a diffusion of myths from Atlantis or the Garden of Eden or the collective unconscious or what not. But we don't need such theories. If we go into a museum, and look at cultural objects from societies all over the world, such as textiles or pottery or masks, we find that the same principles of design keep recurring. Certain blends and contrasts of colors, certain geometrical patterns, will resemble one another even where there is no question of direct influence. There is enough uniformity in the human mind, in the order of nature that that mind works with, and in the physical conditions of the medium itself, to account for all such similarities.

The Function of Archetypes

In one of the books in this series there is a story, told among a tribe of Californian Indians, of a man who followed the shade of his wife to the land of the dead and was allowed to return with her on condition that he did not touch her before they were back home. Anyone familiar with Greek mythology would say, on reading this story: "That is the same story as the story of Orpheus and Eurydice." We notice that there is no question of the Greek story's having influenced the Californian one, or vice versa. Even if there were, the fact that the same story makes an appeal to two such very different cultures would still be significant. But in what sense is it the "same" story? The incidents are different; the journey to the land of the dead is different; there is no mention of the hero as a musician, as Orpheus was, and the taboo is of touching in this story and of looking back in the Greek one. When we say that it is the "same" story, we are speaking of the shape the story assumes when we look at it all at once as a piece of verbal design, after listening to it being told. As something told and listened to, the story is a narrative or plot (the Greek word for plot, *mythos*, is the source of our word *myth*); as something to be studied and compared with other stories like it, it is a theme. As a plot, it moves in time, and our reading of it is also a movement in time. As a theme, it exists all at once in space, like a picture. The Californian Indian story and the Orpheus story are the "same" story because they have the same theme.

We notice that the Californian Indian story incorporates an episode of clashing rocks. That incident is not in the Greek story of Orpheus and Eurydice, but it appears in another Greek story, the voyage of the Argonauts (where Orpheus was also present). This kind of motif, which can appear in any story, is an "archetype," that is, a repeatable unit of imaginative experience that turns up constantly and unpredictably. Just how unpredictable such units can be we can see from this account of the seduction of a girl by a serpent:

> Cinderella dressed in yella
> Went upstairs to kiss her fella.
> Made a mistake and kissed a snake
> And came downstairs with a bellyache.

The verses are nonsense, but amusing nonsense, and no nonsense is amusing if it is *entirely* pointless.

The story of Orpheus and Eurydice is in the center of the western literary tradition, and so hundreds of poets have referred to it and many composers have written operas about it. Consequently it comes to us with the resonance of these echoes around it, as the Indian story does not. But the Indian story, if we listen to it sympathetically, is just as haunting and suggestive, just as touching and as close to our own sense of loneliness and bereavement, as the Greek one. Thus the *quality* of literature does not depend on the technological development of the culture that produced it. Literature does not improve when social conditions improve, or are assumed to improve.

It is true of all forms of human creativity that, while we may in some contexts speak of a development from primitive societies to high civilizations, there is no corresponding development of quality in the arts. Just as the textile or pottery designs of "primitive" peoples may often seem to us as sophisticated as our own, and sometimes much more tasteful, so "primitive" myths and folk tales can be on at least the same imaginative level as our own stories. If we call such stories crude or undeveloped, we are probably misinterpreting them, or thinking of them as early efforts at conceptual thought. They are not forms of conceptual thought at all: they usually come from societies where conceptual thought has no real function. They are forms of imaginative thought, and that can be as subtle and suggestive in the tales of the "eternal dream time" told by Australian aborigines as in our own culture. That is why literature, no less than painting and sculpture, has continually to turn to the primitive, to ballad and popular song and folk tale, to find the sources of its own vitality, and why this literature program makes so much of these sources. Behind these sources, and even more important for us than they are, are the mainsprings of western cultural tradition, the Old Testament and Greek mythology.

The Primacy of Poetry

One of the things we learn, if we study such a people as the Eskimos, for example, whose conditions of life have kept them technologically restricted and close to the subsistence level, is that the simpler the society, the more clearly poetry emerges as one of the primary needs of that society. In a civilization like ours, poetry, like physical exercise, gets smothered under a mass of other activities. We forget how simple and direct a form of expression poetry is: how it is linked to singing and dancing and marching. Like singing and dancing themselves, however, poetry has come to be regarded as a difficult skill attained by very few people. But the three-year-old who learns to hear and repeat nursery rhymes with the kind of rhythmical swing that belongs to them is learning something about the real impact of poetry that many of us have forgotten or never knew. The editors of these books have assumed that the nursery rhymes and fairy tales that children hear in their preschool years, if they are lucky, are the right beginning of a literary education, and they have tried to continue this instead of interrupting it, as school education too often does.

The superstition that poetry is difficult and specialized has produced many anthologies and textbooks based on the assumption that the study of poetry should be either circumvented altogether or approached with the greatest caution, and that prose should be the staple of literary education. A culture like ours, submerged under great masses of print that pass for prose, tends to assume that prose must be the natural way to speak and think. But, if prose is more "natural" than poetry, how does it happen that the simplest and most primitive societies have poetry, whereas prose is always a much later and more specialized development? And, more important for us just now, if prose is the natural way to speak, why do young people, introduced to prose in the early grades of school, treat it as a dead language, with no relation whatever to the way that they actually do speak? And why is it that even at the university, by which time the propaganda has done its work and students have finally become convinced that prose is the natural way to write and speak, they still cannot write it, and never speak it consistently?

The truth of the matter is, first, that the natural way to speak is not in prose, despite the pleasure of M. Jourdain in Molière at being told that he had been speaking prose all his life. The natural way to speak is in an associative and repetitive babble which is neither prose nor verse. If we want to see what it looks like in print, we should read Gertrude Stein, the one twentieth-century writer who has completely mastered its peculiar idiom. Verse and prose are different ways of regulating and controlling this babble, but prose is a far more difficult and sophisticated way of conventionalizing speech than verse is. It is therefore better and more logical teaching to begin with poetry, and keep it at the center of all one's training in literature. And, if we once understand the primitive and simple nature of the rhythm of poetry as compared with prose, we may go on to understand something of the primitive and simple nature of its use of language and its methods of thought. The poet, like the child, is dependent on sense experience rather than abstraction, and his primary units of expression are images, not ideas or concepts. Poetry has a limited tolerance for abstractions of any kind, including the abstractions of critical commentary.

Image: The Unit of Meaning

Again, the poet thinks, not in logical sequences, but in the most primitive and archaic of categories, similarity and identity: A is like B; A is B. These are the categories that appear in poetry as simile and metaphor. "Eternity is like unto a Ring," says John Bunyan; "Grandfather of the day is he," says Emily Dickinson of a mountain. The program begins with riddles, describing things in terms of other things:

As round as an apple,
As deep as a cup,
And all the king's horses
Cannot pull it up.

Such poetry makes a direct appeal to the intellectual excitement of childhood: the child wants to "guess," and thereby he recapitulates the whole history of literature, where the riddle, along with the riddle game and the riddle duel, is among the most ancient of poetic forms. In fact "riddle" was originally what one "read." I suppose no poetry will ever be written more difficult and elusive than that of the nineteenth-century French poet Mallarmé, yet Mallarmé's prescription for writing poetry, to describe, not the thing, but the effect it produces, is still essentially a prescription for writing riddles. Such mental processes as those that are involved in riddles, proceeding through pun and identification, are very close to the mental processes of young children. A generation ago T. S. Eliot said that poets writing in so unpoetic a time as ours have a moral obligation to be difficult. But a proper literary education would preserve a child's own metaphorical processes not distort them in the interests of a false notion of reality. If it did, the child would grow up to find the most apparently difficult poetry a simple, direct, natural, even inevitable form of expression.

Literature is produced by, and appeals to, the imagination. The imagination is a creative and constructive power: it is different from reason, though it is intelligent, and different from feeling, though it is sensitive. If we are responding to someone else's poem, we should respond to it at first with intelligence and feeling, as we do to anything else outside ourselves. But sooner or later we come up against the question of how our own powers of creation can be related to what the poet has made. For, however unlikely it is that we could make anything like *King Lear* or *Paradise Lost,* our response even to that level of creation still has in it some quality of recognition. Lear on the heath is not like anything we have actually experienced, either in waking life or in dreams. Nevertheless he reminds us that besides actual worlds and fantasy worlds, we do have an imaginative world of our own, a world of possibilities, so to speak, and that Lear is within range of something that we can imagine. We know very little about our own imaginative worlds: even a great genius may not know much about what his genius is producing. Hence we are, at least at first, totally inarticulate about what we can imagine, until something in literature, say a poem, comes along and expresses it. Then we realize that that poem corresponds to something in a world that we have lived in and lived with, but knew nothing about until the poem spoke for us.

This imaginative world that remains within us, hidden and mysterious, until literature begins to call it forth, is a world with a shape to it. We have just said that each work of literature has a context within literature: it lights up a specific corner or area of our imaginative experience, and the other works of literature that are most like it are in neighboring areas. The editors of these books have taken the logical next step, and have tried to sketch out for the student the outlines of his own imaginative world. That sounds at first like a formidable undertaking, but the two main principles involved are very simple.

The Two Rhythms of Literature

First, the easiest way to impose artistic shape on material is to give it a recurring pattern. For arts that move in time, like poetry and music, this means the repetition of an established rhythm. The poet uses words, and it is not too difficult to put words into regular rhythm. But words, unlike musical notes, have to mean something besides their own sound: they also describe and refer to the world around us, or, as critics back to Plato have said, they imitate nature. The first thing poetry does, in transforming "nature" into an imaginative world, is to seize on the element of regular repetition in it.

This is the element provided by the cyclical rhythm of nature: the four seasons of the year moving from spring to winter and back to spring again; the daily cycle of the sun moving from dawn to darkness to a new dawn, the cycle of waters running into the sea and returning in the rain. Next comes the fact referred to above, that the poet thinks in terms of likeness and identity. And what likeness and identity suggest is adding to the cycle of nature the rhythm of life, with human life at its center, moving from birth to death and back again to new life. But this step gets our own emotions immediately involved with the cycle. And as poetry continues to express not merely the rhythm of what we see around us but what we feel as a part of ourselves, a second principle begins to operate, a principle which tends to separate what we hate or fear from what we want or love. Out of this cycle of death and renewal, and out of the separation of our feelings about the cycle, there gradually emerge four fundamental types of imaginative experience in literature. The editors call this sequence of four types, the first time they appear, the "circle of stories." Later they are referred to by their more usual names: romance, tragedy, irony, and comedy.

Romance is the name we give to the type of imaginative literature that takes place in an idealized or stylized world inhabited by brave men and beautiful women, where all villains are easy to recognize as villainous. Such a world is likely to be considerably simplified in its setting also: the discomforts, frustrations, and confusions of ordinary life are largely cleared away. Opposed to romance is the world explored in irony and satire: this is much closer to the world we live in, except that irony puts us in a position of some superiority to the characters in the story, though not so much as to prevent us from being involved with the story. It will generally be found, however, that the shape of an ironic story often takes the form of a parody of romance, as stories of adventurous voyages are parodied in *Gulliver's Travels* and stories of knights rescuing maidens and the like are parodied in *Don Quixote*.

Then there are the stories we call comedies and tragedies, the stories that turn up or turn down at the end. Tragedy usually focuses on a hero, a central figure of more than ordinary size, who is caught in a situation that propels him inevitably into disaster, whether death or a loss of freedom of action. The direction of the tragic plot is thus from the romantic to the ironic. Comedy moves in the opposite direction, from a condition where (to take a very common type of comedy) a hero and heroine are threatened with separation or a loss of freedom by some obsessed or ridiculous character, but manage to evade all obstacles and proceed to a happy conclusion, often marriage. Thus comedy normally moves from the ironic to the romantic worlds. But a tragedy may have its center of gravity, so to speak, in romance, like *Romeo and Juliet*, or in irony, like *Death of a Salesman*, as a comedy may be centered in irony (ironic comedy is generally called satire), like *Vanity Fair*, or in romance, like *The Tempest*.

We may feel that this "circle of stories" considerably simplifies the facts of literary experience. Three points in this connection are important. First, the simplification may be valuable for teaching purposes, giving shape and coherence to an inexperienced student's reading. Second, no boundary lines exist, except in diagrams: no classifying or pigeonholing is involved; literary works are simply seen as being in different areas, where they can be both distinguished from and related to one another. Third, and most important, this is not a schematism to be imposed on students. The teacher should have it in mind, but as a principle to give form to his teaching, not as something for the student to memorize and present as a substitute for literary experience.

We come then at least to the beginning of an answer to the question of what we should teach. We should teach literature, but in such a way that the primary facts emerge first, and the primary experiences are properly emphasized, so that whatever the student goes on to next will be continuous with what he has already experienced. That implies teaching the structure of literature, and the content by means of the structure, so that the content can be seen to have some reason in the structure for existing. Very often literary materials in schoolbooks are arranged by content, by what they say about love or time or death or what not. When well done, such an approach may overlap with the present one: putting poems on spring together is to some extent arrangement by content too. But the approach of this program also provides a containing form for the themes: love and death are not taken as real classifying principles, but as aspects of literary genres, such as comedy and tragedy. This avoids the danger of classifying literature by what it says, and so making literary works into documents illustrating various Noble Notions. It thus avoids the moralizing of literature, of treating it as a collection of allegories of something else. Moral and allegorical approaches to imaginative literature have been experimented with from classical times down through the Middle Ages and Renaissance to the "Synopticon" of a few years ago, which attempted to present all the great ideas of man in reference form. But somehow or other this approach has never really worked, except when the moral principles mainly featured were also those that the power structure of society was determined to enforce. It has not worked because it does not follow the actual shape of literature, but distorts that shape in the interests of something else.

Myth and the Imagination

Every society has a verbal culture, which includes ballads, folk songs, folk tales, work songs, legends, and the like. As it develops, a special group of stories, the stories we call myths, begins to crystallize in the center of this verbal culture. These stories are taken with particular seriousness by their society, because they express something deep in that society's beliefs or vision of its situation and destiny. Myths, unlike other types of stories, stick together to form a mythology, and this mythology begins to take on the outlines of the imaginative world just described. Creation myths and other myths that account for the origins of things appear at one end of it, and myths of a final dissolving or transforming of the world may appear at the other, though this is normally a later development. Literature as we know it, as a body of writing, always develops out of a mythical framework of this kind. The heaven or paradise or Mount Olympus of the mythology becomes the idealized world of romance and pastoral and idyl, and its hell or Tartarus or Hades becomes the abhorred or grotesque world of irony.

The mythological framework of western culture has been provided mainly by the Bible, with the mythology of Greece and Rome forming a counterpoint against it. During the last century or so we have been learning more and more about the similarity of these mythical patterns to those produced by other societies all over the world, which, of course, in itself gives the study of literature an important function in a world where we have to meet so many other peoples on their terms as well as ours. The present literature program is full of mythical stories from a wide variety of sources, and their similarity to more familiar ones is clear enough. But, as we said above, the biblical and classical versions are the ones that western poets have known: they are the ones with literary echoes around them, and they have an obvious priority in western literary education.

Of course the fact that the Bible has been traditionally associated with belief, and that classical mythology has not, at least not since the rise of Christianity, makes for differences in emphasis. There has been a long-standing notion that poets are just playing with words, and novelists just telling stories for fun. Hence the writer comes to be thought of as a kind of licensed liar, and the words for literary structure, *fable*, *fiction*, and *myth*, acquire a secondary sense in which they simply mean something untrue. This provides quite a hurdle for the study of literature to get over. When I became a junior instructor in English many years ago, I began a course on the imagery and symbolism of the Bible, which I am still teaching. I thought, as I still think, that without some knowledge of the Bible one simply does not know what is going on in English literature. Also that while the Bible may be many things besides a work of literature, it must be that too, as no book can have had its influence on literature without itself having literary qualities. Naturally some of my students found it hard to understand why poets did not confine themselves to classical mythology, where they could do what they liked, instead of meddling with really serious issues. To demonstrate that poets took their work very seriously was not difficult, but there was another set of objections when I carried the campaign into the opposite camp, and began calling biblical stories myths, and biblical images metaphors. The questions usually took some such form as "Do you mean to say that it's all just a myth, only a myth, nothing but a myth?" Here one had to explain that, in the first place, a myth is a certain kind of story, and that calling a biblical story a myth is simply making a statement about its form or mode of presentation, not about the reality or unreality of its content. Secondly, that the Bible employs myth and metaphor because it expects the active and constructive response from its readers that only the imagination gives. The fact that Jesus taught in parables and stories obviously increases the seriousness and immediacy of what he had to say.

In the last few years students have started to ask very different questions. They are, after all, living in an age where it is all too easy to see that anything, religious or scientific, becomes dangerous to society as soon as it is uncritically accepted. Whenever we try to place any subject beyond criticism, what we are really placing beyond criticism is our present understanding of that subject. The motivation for religious persecution, for instance, is never "You must believe in God," but "You must believe what I mean by God." The next step is to understand that what is real or true about any human form of understanding, whether religion or philosophy or science or literature, is not its relation to objective fact, but its relation to our own power to use it. So it is reassuring to find that students now seem to realize that active imagination is worth any amount of passive faith.

Models for Action

There is, however, a still more important principle involved here, so far as the teaching of literature is concerned. Every belief or doctrine which can be expressed as a general statement or proposition is also the moral of a possible story. Literature addresses itself to the imagination, and the imagination is not directly related to belief. It is concerned rather with models of possible belief, structures which may be "just stories" in their literary form, but may also take on the outlines of a much wider and more comprehensive social vision. What we believe is not what we think we believe but what our actions show that we believe. Our actions in their turn are chosen by a certain kind of social vision, and if we were sufficiently conscious of our social vision to describe it, we should find it taking on the outlines of a story and a body of imagery.

One of the stories in this program is of a medieval baron who is a werewolf, and is forced to become a wolf for three days each week. His wife, who wants to marry someone else, worms his secret out of him (Samson-Delilah archetype), steals his clothes so that he cannot become human again, marries the other man, and takes over his property. The king goes out hunting, finds the wolf, and the wolf proves so affectionate that he spares his life and takes him back to the court. Eventually the whole story comes out: the baron is restored to his normal shape, and the lady and her second husband are baffled. Just a story, and a very simple and childlike story at that. Yet the structural device employed is an extremely common one in literature, which implies that it belongs to a fairly important group of structures. In Homer's *Odyssey*, for example, the hero remains absent from home while other suitors of his wife lay waste his goods; he returns secretly and in disguise, and eventually reveals his true shape and destroys the suitors. In Shakespeare's *Measure for Measure* the Duke of Vienna disappears, leaving a regent in charge, returns secretly, disguised as a friar, and finally reveals his true shape, to the great discomfiture of the regent, who has not been behaving well.

There are no greater writers than Shakespeare or Homer, but still, we may feel, these are "just stories," told to amuse. But then we may begin to think about, say, the teachings of Christianity, which form not only a body of doctrines but a story. The story tells how Christ leaves the world after his ascent to heaven, returns in secret to the human heart, often neglected or ignored and his authority usurped, yet to be finally revealed in a second coming at the end of time. The story of Christianity, we see, is, from the literary point of view, a comedy: that is what the greatest of Christian poets, Dante, called it. Then there is Marxism, which turns on the theme of a usurping ascendant class getting the benefits of society while an oppressed class remains hidden within it, some day to manifest itself in full force and to return to its rights. In short, hundreds of millions of people today are thinking about the world within the kind of framework represented by that werewolf story.

Literature in the Free Society

The social importance of teaching literature, then, does not stop, as so many people think it does, when children have acquired the skills of reading and writing. Nobody denies the importance of these skills: all social participation depends on them. But in themselves they are passive skills: the knowledge of how to read leads in itself merely to reading such things as traffic signs, to learning how to do what one is told. If we go on with the study of literature, it turns out to be, not something to fill in our spare time with, but an organization of human experience. It presents the human situation, not as we ordinarily know it, as a dissolving flux, but in structured forms like romance, tragedy, irony, comedy. To reach this kind of transformed imaginative reality, its rhythms have to be more concentrated, its imagery bolder, and its conventions at once more stylized and more varied, than anything we can use for ordinary experience. Literature in this sense is cultural mythology, the social vision which is not in itself belief or action, but the imaginative reservoir out of which beliefs and actions come.

Every subject worth teaching is also a militant subject, fighting against the social perversion of itself. To teach science is implicitly to fight against mental confusion and superstition; to teach geography and history is implicity to fight against provincialism. And as we continue to study literature, we begin to realize that every society also produces a social mythology, or what is often called an ideology, that it has techniques of ensuring that its citizens learn it thoroughly and early, and that literature has the social function of trying to clarify and provide imaginative standards for this ideology.

There are two aspects of social mythology. One is its genuine aspect, as the body of beliefs or feelings that are held deeply, if often very inarticulately, by a society. American social mythology, for instance, has a concern for self-reliance and independence, for tolerance (which is really intellectual independence), for the democratic process, for an inclusive community that does not make second-class citizens out of any group. This mythology, like other mythologies, is a construct of historically chosen beliefs and principles, and is incorporated in the Constitution. The fact that it is a mythology, once more, does not mean that it is untrue, but that its truth depends on the way it is used. A great American writer, such as Whitman or Thoreau, will almost always be found to have struck his roots deeply into it. But there is also a strong tendency to project this mythology, to treat it as a body of established social principles, to be imposed on everyone without criticism. This produces a mythology which aims at conditioning all citizens in habits of docility and obedience, or, as it is called, adjustment.

This projected adjustment mythology may be studied in all anthologies and textbooks which assumed that the main function of education is to produce docile citizens. For several generations it was widely assumed that the student should learn as much of this adjustment mythology as possible, and as little as possible of anything else. In fact the study of this mythology frequently replaced the study of actual literature. The mythology in the United States presented a nostalgic version of the American past, with certain mythical figures looming out of it, some named, like Franklin and Washington, and some general, like the pioneer, the hunter, and the cowboy. The present was a middle-class world of comfort and security, where the main outlet for adventure was in operating the technological machinery. The rest of the world, including the rest of the United States, hardly existed at all, or existed only among certain exotic peoples who were to be tolerated and sympathized with, but of course at a distance. So far as it addressed itself to literature, it tended to vulgarize the imaginative response to literature, so as to make the student a part of the captive audience of the mass media in their present facile commercialized form.

The result was all too often to train the student in stock response, not imagination, and the end of the process to get him in adult life to repeat the liturgy of the adjustment myth, in a series of cliché-notions that show traces of the Christian myth from which it was, at many removes, derived. We have all heard these clichés: things were much simpler in the old days; the world has unaccountably lost its innocence since I was a child; I just live to get out of this rat race for a while and go somewhere where I can get away from it all; there is a bracing atmosphere in progress and competition, and although the world is threatened with grave dangers from foreigners, yet if we dedicate ourselves anew to the tasks before us we may preserve the American way of life for generations yet unborn. One recognizes the dim outlines of pastoral myths, fall-from-Paradise myths, exodus-from-Egypt myths, and apocalyptic myths. Genuine American mythology, we said, stresses independence, tolerance, and personal freedom. But no adjustment myth can possibly believe in such things: if it did it would cease to become an adjustment myth. It has to present such beliefs as ways of getting along in a benevolently authoritarian social establishment. Thus the belief in independence and individuality gradually turns into an acceptance of the power of a pervasive but almost invisible corporate state. More important for our present purposes is the principle involved, that if we neglect or misunderstand the teaching of literature, we create a vacuum in education, and adjustment mythology rushes in to fill the empty space. We have no choice about teaching mythology; we have only the choice between teaching genuine and perverted kinds of it.

The Imaginative vs. the Imaginary

One trouble with the stock-response version of literary teaching is that this kind of education is performed far more expertly by advertising, especially television commercials. Advertising, being a socially approved form of drug culture, envelops us in an imaginary world, and promises us magical powers within that world enabling us to transcend the world we actually live in. As we grow older, we learn not to take this very seriously, but we acquire the habit of responding to advertising in childhood, and if we simply outgrow it, many of the elements in that response will remain with us. It seems to me that the study of literature should be accompanied, as early as possible, by the study of the rhetorical devices of advertising, propaganda, official releases, news media, and everything else in a citizen's verbal experience that he is compelled to confront but is not (so far in our society) compelled to believe, or say he believes. The rhetorical devices of advertising are easily analyzed, and such analysis uncovers a primitive level of verbal response that literature as such cannot reach. In totalitarian states advertising turns into propaganda, and the element of competition, which, along with the separation of economic and political establishments, makes advertising something of an ironic game, disappears. The fact that first-rate literature also disappears in totalitarian states is part of the same process.

Literature, as ordinarily conceived, is so small and specialized a part of one's reading that we forget how much of our total verbal experience is untouched by it. For many a student in grade eight whose verbal experience is centered on television, *The Lady of the Lake* may be a pretty meaningless collection of words, something that those unaccountable adults, for whatever reasons of their own, think he should read. The way out of this is not to try to choose the kind of literature that can compete with the appeal of television—no such literature exists. But the teacher should understand that teaching literature means dealing with the total verbal experience of students. The points of contact between literary and subliterary experiences should be kept in mind; obviously the same forms of comedy and romance and irony that appear in literature also turn up in television drama or rock ballads. I am not saying that a teacher should be constantly pointing such resemblances out, only that they are occasionally useful. Far more important, however, is the fact that students are being steadily got at by a rival mythology determined to capture their imaginations for its own purposes, armed with far more skill, authority, and prestige than any teacher has. This is why I think students should be encouraged to become aware of the extent to which they are being conditioned by the mass media, as a central part of their literary training. Some of them have reacted with a general hatred and contempt for everything their society produces, but that, of course, is quite as dependent on conditioned reflex as anything it revolts against. Besides, it does not distinguish between genuine and false forms of social mythology. What is absurd about growing up absurd is adjustment mythology, not society itself.

If I am asked how we should teach, therefore, I should begin by saying that the sense of urgent necessity about learning to read and write should never drop out of the teaching of literature, at any stage. We cannot take any part in a society as verbal as ours without knowing how to read and write: but, unless we also learn to read continuously, selectively, and critically, and to write articulately, we can never take any free or independent part in that society. As we gradually become more aware that what we do and believe is the product of a social vision, we can see that this social vision is a product of the imagination. As such, it has been developed by our imaginative experience. Some of this has been formed by literature, but by far the greater part of it has been formed on the subliterary level of mass media and the like. The social importance of literature, in this context, is that it helps us to become aware of the extent to which we are acting out a social mythology. Part of this awareness is in realizing that there is a good deal of it that we don't really believe or respect, but are merely following out of habit and laziness.

When Flaubert wrote *Bouvard and Pecuchet*, an account of two cliché-ridden French bourgeoisie, he also drew up a "Dictionary of Accepted Ideas" to indicate the limitations of their culture. The dictionary arrangement of course conceals the fact that the accepted ideas form a mythology. *Madame Bovary* is much clearer on this point: it shows how Emma Bovary's life was dominated by the shoddy construct that her imagination had built, mainly out of subliterary sources. The people who want to censor everything have got one thing right: they do see that what addresses our imaginations does influence our lives, for good or for evil. But, apart from being mistaken in their tactics, they are nearly always on the side of bad social mythology rather than of genuine literature, and consequently it is genuine literature that they usually want most of all to attack.

2

Theory into Practice: Pursuing Hidden Likenesses

WHENEVER WE READ ANYTHING, whatever it is, we find our attention going in two directions at once. One direction is centrifugal, where we are associating each word we read with our memory of what it conventionally means. We may hardly realize we are doing this, but if we are reading something in a language we barely know, so that we have to look up a word every so often, we soon become aware of how important this direction is. I call it centrifugal because it moves outside what we are reading into our memories, or, if we don't know the word, into dictionaries. At the same time there is a direction of attention going the other way, centripetally, where we are fitting the words in what we are reading together. When Sandburg writes

> The fog comes
> on little cat feet

we remember what a cat is and what feet are, but we also have to know why these words are brought into a poem about a fog. Meaning is derived from context. The context of the dictionary meaning of *cat* is different from the context in Sandburg's poem, but the meaning of *cat* in that poem is at the point of intersection, so to speak, of the two contexts.

Now, suppose we are reading something specifically for imaginative pleasure, as a poem or story or the like. That means that what we are reading has a special context outside it called, however vaguely, literature. What we are reading is *like* other "literary" things we have read. I gave an example of this a while ago, when we found elements in a Californian Indian story that reminded us of similar things in Greek stories. Whenever we find something in one piece of literature that reminds us irresistibly of something in another piece of literature, we have found what we have been calling an archetype. If a reader who knows very little English has to look up *cat* and *feet* in Sandburg's poem, he will have two useful words in expanding his mastery of the language in general. Similarly, whenever we pursue the likenesses in what we are reading, we are beginning to expand our mastery and knowledge of literature. That is, perhaps, the most distinctive feature of the present program: that students should be encouraged to pursue the resemblances in what they read.

It may be thought that this practice will require a great deal of erudition. But it should be realized, first of all, that what the teacher of literature is concerned with is the total verbal experience of his students. That includes conversation with families and classmates, movies and television, comic books and advertising. For all important archetypes, a teacher can start wherever his students are, and any question of the "What does this remind you of?" type will soon produce all the examples he can handle for some time. In *Wish and Nightmare* there is a telling of the Jack-the-giant-killer story. If we try this out on a junior high school class (as teachers have done: this is not simply theory), somebody may be reminded of the David and Goliath story in the Bible or the story of Odysseus and Polyphemus in Homer. But there will also be a flood of analogies from other sources that show how archetypes are not at all confined to what we normally think of as literature. Sergeant York, up against a German platoon. Truman winning an election over Dewey after all the polls and news commentators had decided that it was in the bag for Dewey. Clark Kent turning into Superman. Aspirin defeating Headache in a television commercial. The wise teacher will not reject these as not being literary. They are literary enough to address the imagination, and they are part of the student's total verbal experience. The next question could be: Why is the audience's sympathy usually with Jack rather than the giant? Again there will be no lack of answers. People like to see the little guy win. People like to see brains beat muscles. It's more unexpected and exciting to see the little fellow come out on top. Nobody likes bullies. Such answers are not just reflections about life: they are answers that take us deep into the structure of comedy and romance.

We notice that several of the examples given above illustrate some aspects of the archetypes and not others. Some suggestions may be too far away to be very useful, because in literature there is an immense amount of general and vague resemblance. The teacher's experience and guidance come into play in emphasizing the examples that illustrate rather than digress. In the same book there is the story of "Ashpet," or Cinderella. Some students may suggest that Cinderella and Jack are parallel, that Cinderella is really a female Jack. But with a little more discussion it will become clear that the two stories are quite distinct in both structure and feeling, though, of course, they are related within the general area of comic romance. Discovering analogies is fun, but discovering differences provides direction. Accepting the student's verbal experience as it is is the first step in transforming the teacher-student relationship into a common participation in the subject.

Of all the perverted adjustment myths dealt with above, one of the most pervasive is the myth which rationalizes the subordinating of some group of people in society. In Victorian times, for example, women were made the focus of certain social anxieties. Their sensibilities, which were assumed to be exceedingly delicate, formed an imaginary criterion for society's constant dread of an unregulated sexual instinct, and for the enforcing of social standards connected with that dread, such as those which were assumed in the censorship of books. We remember Podsnap in Dickens's *Our Mutual Friend*, and his appeal to the blushing cheeks of the young person. Podsnap was not alone: even Tennyson could be seriously praised for never having written a line that would distress a sensitive female. This was part of a social code of allegedly sheltering and protecting the delicate sex from the rougher facts of life, in the middle class at any rate. But on the excuse of protecting womanhood, women were deprived of equal participation in society, not allowed to vote, or even to own property after they were married. We may look also at the way that blacks used to be treated in a good deal of popular white literature, as comic-strip characters who were generally good-natured and lovable, but not very strong on intellect. The implication of such writing was that, blacks being naturally just happy children, they wouldn't worry too much about being excluded from full participation in society. It looks as though the instinct to patronize and the instinct to exploit are rather closely related. This is not hard to see in, for instance, the African and Asian colonies developed by western powers during the nineteenth century: it has taken a little longer to understand how disastrous the working of such complacent mythologies in our own society can be.

It is most important to realize that we have been applying a very similar mythology to young people for the last three or four generations at least, and that the results have been equally explosive. The motive has been not so much exploitation as the dramatizing of an aspect of the social mythology referred to above. We remember that that mythology contained a pastoral, or primal-Paradise, myth. When people become adults, old enough to vote and hold jobs, they become involved in a social rat race, full of cares and worries and responsibilities. When they look back to their childhood, they reconstruct it as a world which was happier because it had less responsibility. Children, then, should be protected from the adult world as long as possible: why make them old before their time? School is there to keep them off the streets not only physically but mentally: the young should be in a special preserved world, like the Garden of Eden before the Fall. Most innocent worlds, including the Garden of Eden, are presexual worlds, hence books for younger people, especially schoolbooks, have to be ruthlessly, even hysterically, censored to remove any trace of a specific reference to the way that human life keeps going. Nobody is fool enough actually to believe that a young person's life is sexless, but books for the young have for a long time been expurgated as though this were true, in order to preserve the myth for the reassurance of adults.

Genuine Literature for Real People

"Adolescence," in short, is not really a process that young people must all go through. A great deal of it is really a deliberate creation of adult social anxieties.

In order to maintain the adult dream of a happy clean world of fun-loving middle-class children, we have to assume that a person takes twenty-odd years to grow into a genuine human being. During this period, everything he is "not ready for" should be kept from him, which in practice tends to mean that all genuine education should be postponed as long as possible, as explained above. Whatever is socially undesirable, such as violence, is also to be kept from him, on the theory, if that is the word, that if he never reads about violence it cannot occur to him to become violent. Sex and violence, therefore, come to be associated with adult books, the books one reads outside of school or after one has finished school, which is a major reason why the popular taste in reading, and entertainment generally, whether adolescent or adult, is so prurient and sadistic. I think a little more emphasis on genuine literature in school might make this tendency less automatic.

It is, of course, quite as easy for young people as it has been for women and blacks to see through the trick. They realize that what all the coddling and permissiveness really means is exclusion from serious social issues, and from any real participation in society. What is important is not so much to keep them in school as to keep them off the labor market. An overproductive economy would like to turn all children, as it would like to turn all women, into full-time consumers. And no matter how much "citizenship" young people may study, or how much they may learn about democratic processes, the fundamentally antidemocratic attitude of protection which surrounds them from infancy nullifies all this, and throws them on the world expecting more protection. This issue, which has always been serious, has reached a crisis with the coming of television. In an age of electronic media it is no use going on with the pretense that young people in their teens can be kept in a world by themselves. As we have already seen during the past few years, people who have no social function quickly get bored, and boredom leads to smashing things.

Although the literature program is addressed to a specific age level, and uses material appropriate to that level, it does not condescend to its readers. There is no feeling of "this is all you are ready for at present" hanging around it. This program covers the same area that adult literature covers, including the tragic and the ironic, not a special preserve fenced off within it. There are also stories by and about black and Indian groups indicating that American society and middle-class white American society are not the same thing. What the young student is "not ready for" may be more complex, like the later novels of Henry James or the poetry of Wallace Stevens, but it is not different in kind. Whatever else he reads, at the same time or later, can be seen to be continuous with what is presented to him here. Anyone, at any time of life, may become demoralized by the sense that the world is very different from what he had been told it was. But no teacher wants to feel involved in a process of systematically lying to young people. And while no book can be ideal, even for a single reader, I think that the books in this program are ones that students themselves will respond to eagerly. Some people may object to exposing "our children" to so many serious, even tragic and ironic, themes, and some may believe that children should be taught, in effect, nothing except what they cannot help discovering for themselves, hence such material as these books present is fantastically difficult. The difficulty is for them, not the students, and consists of panic and mental block, not of anything actually in the books.

The Authority of the Subject

The title of a book in the program already available is *Wish and Nightmare.* The title is significant in itself of the change which has come over social assumptions in the last generation. We understand better now how much "nightmare" comes into life at every age. Nightmares enter the life of the youngest child, to such an extent that it is no good trying to remove them from his experience, for nightmare is not something presented to us from outside: it is something that our own minds construct. The sound of children at play is often regarded, by those bemused with the paradisal myth of childhood, as the sound of the purest and most innocent happiness, but anyone who listens carefully to it, and to the amount of hysteria and aggression in it, can see that the facts of life are otherwise. The way to deal with nightmare, educationally, is not to pretend that it is not or need not be there, or, as in some of the more brutal movies and thrillers, to force it on us on the pretext that "society is involved with it," but to present it in its real context, the context of irony, where it can be seen with detachment, as the vision we must have of the world that we don't want.

As for "wish" we have also discovered that that is a far more powerful element in life than we used to think. Wishing used to be thought of as a natural but helpless reaction against "reality," including in that term both the objective world of nature and certain social conditions that men have made themselves. But clearly anything that men have made can be unmade by other men, and in the last few years there has been a dramatic development of the sense that wishing can be a concrete and revolutionary force: that we don't have to live with the mistakes of the past if we don't want to. Again, this feeling need not take the form of a querulous pseudoradical demand for everything to be much better right away, or some vague hope that an inspired political leader will somehow put everything right, but should be studied in its proper context, the context of comedy, or the vision of how desire is not always frustrated by reality, but is sometimes strong enough to transform reality, and force things to turn out better than habit and inertia had expected.

If we ask whom we should teach, then, the beginning of the answer is that we teach mainly young people, but we teach them as people and not as a special kind of people. Still less do we teach them as half-developed people who must be kept away from what real people, that is, adults, talk about. This sounds obvious to the verge of being offensive, but the implications of the attitude go a little farther. The emphasis on teaching by personal relationships has much that is good in it, along with much that is merely addled, if well-meaning. While many things can bring teacher and students together personally, only one thing can ever *equalize* them, and that is the authority of the subject being taught. In relation to the subject being taught the teacher is also a student, and so the difference between teacher and students is at a minimum. The role of teacher vis-à-vis the students has its embarrassing aspects for both, and every genuine moment of insight in a classroom carries with it a sense of momentary relief from that embarrassment. When either teacher or students dominate a classroom, there are, of course, likely to be very few such moments. When they do occur, they are moments when the one real authority in the classroom is supreme over both, and everyone is united in the vision of its power.

The Reality of Metaphor

The student of literature is continually being brought back to the passage in Shakespeare's *Midsummer Night's Dream* in which Duke Theseus classifies poets with lunatics and lovers as being "of imagination all compact." These three groups are, in the first place, the only people who can take metaphor seriously. The "lunatic" is normally obsessed by some kind of identification, usually of himself with something or someone else; lovers desire, in Sir Thomas Browne's phrase, "to be truly each other," and poets assert, or seem to be asserting, like Lady Lowzen in Wallace Stevens's poem "Oak Leaves Are Hands," that what is is other things. We notice that this progression moves from the negative through the playful to the positive. The same thing is true of another characteristic of these three groups: that they seem to be unable to distinguish fiction from fact. The lunatic, that is, anyone so disturbed mentally or emotionally that he needs help in managing his own affairs, is the prisoner of his own fictions, which he insists on substituting for the world he is in. The fiction need not be his own creation: anyone who believed advertising literally, for example, would be for all practical purposes a lunatic. Whenever a social mythology is accepted as something beyond criticism, it becomes a fiction or construct taken as fact, and so creates a form of social neurosis. The neurosis may be mild, as it is when criticism and dissent are still tolerated, or acute, as it is when they are suppressed. Here again, the confusion between fiction and fact is negative: one is unable to recognize either, or any distinction between them. We move into a more playful area with the lover: if he asserts that he loves the most wonderful girl in the world, we recognize that some illusions are not only more important than some realities, but may also be truer in the context of personal truth.

When the poet presents us with a work of fiction, and insists, again, that if not literal fact it is still truer than fact, he is giving us the positive side of the identifying of the two. He also raises a good many questions that are harder to answer than they look. The traditional, common-sense view is that literature is an imitation of life, or reality, or nature, or whatever we may think of as outside it, and owes what truth it has to its relation to whatever is not literature. The reversed thesis of Oscar Wilde's *Decay of Lying*, that life imitates literature, and is not real life unless it resembles a literary form, is more recent, but is something much more than just the clever paradox it seems to be. We notice, for example, that we are continually playing roles in society. We are reading by ourselves, let us say: a friend comes in to talk to us, and we instantly throw ourselves into the social role suggested by his presence. Or we decide to maintain a certain public attitude, say in politics, and find that everything we say, or even believe, is being carefully selected by ourselves to fit the role demanded by that attitude. Some psychologists call this role-playing aspect of ourselves a *persona* or mask. But, as the soliloquies of Hamlet remind us, we dramatize ourselves to ourselves, and the mask never really comes off. At present there is a great vogue for "unstructured" personal encounters in which it is believed that we can get past the persona to our "real" attitudes. But there are no real attitudes of this kind: there is never anything under a persona except another persona. It follows that we spend our entire lives playing roles, and are never in any situation which is not to some degree a structured and dramatic situation.

The feeling that there is a "real" self underneath the persona is a tribute to something important, however. It is a part of sanity to be aware that we are playing roles, and a part of our larger freedom to understand what shape those roles have, and why we are adopting them. Looking over some of the books I have been reading recently, I find a book on existential philosophy that said, in effect, "the human situation is tragic," a book on religion (by Kierkegaard) that said, in effect, "God is ironic," and a book on Marxism that said, in effect, "the historical process is a romantic comedy." It is clear that the study of literature has a good deal of usefulness in clarifying such attitudes: none of the authors seemed to realize that his argument was also a literary fiction. Poets are often more versatile. Socrates devoted his life mainly to ironic roles, and Byron to romantic ones, yet Byron wrote satire and Socrates fought with great courage in battle: they were not prisoners of their roles.

The fallacy about the "real self" is of a different kind, and important for our conception of education. Most of us are brought up in a half-baked Rousseauism which makes the individual prior to society. On this theory, the more we explore the hidden or suppressed parts of ourselves, the deeper we are getting into the individual, and the closer we come to the real core of him. But clearly we belong socially before we are individually: if we are born twentieth-century middle-class white Americans, for example, that context is given us long before birth. Below the social comes the generic, what we share with all other human beings. If I know the intimate details of another's sex life, I know only something that is generic about him; if I glimpse his suppressed resentments and aggressions, I see only the aspect of him that can become part of a mob. Individuality is the visible part of the iceberg, the last part of ourselves to be achieved. Our opinions on poetry, music, religion, politics; our relations with one another that deserve the names of friendship or love—these are the things that are individual about us. Individuality, which is the condition of freedom, is never achieved without some genuine form of education. There are of course many forms of that outside the schools, but still there is infinitely more reality, and infinitely more to be discovered about our real selves, in encounter groups with Shakespeare or Milton or Tolstoy than merely with one another.

Relevance to What?

What I have been trying to explain is, to use a vulgarized word in what for me is something close to its proper sense, the "relevance" of teaching literature. Relevance implies a relation to something else, but the question of what relevance is relevant to is often not raised. It seems to me obvious that any subject taught and studied is a part of the whole of human life, and its relevance is to that wholeness. There is no such thing as inherent or built-in relevance; no subject is relevant in itself, because every field of knowledge is equally the center of all knowledge. Relevance is a quality which teachers and students alike bring to a subject of study, and it consists in a vision of the human possibilities connected with that subject. Some subjects, such as car-driving, are obviously and immediately useful; for those that are not, such as the arts and sciences, the question of usefulness moves from an actual into a potential world. They are useful for living a genuinely human life, but of course one can neither prove that a genuinely human life is better than other kinds, or that a certain program of study will necessarily enable one to live it. Teaching is not magic, and it would be a very impudent or self-deceived charlatan who would assert that if we only teach literature properly, certain social benefits are bound to follow. Still, a sense of the worthwhileness of what he is doing is what keeps a teacher going, and surely that sense should be made as specific as possible. If he teaches science, he is trying also to teach intellectual honesty, accuracy, the importance of relying on evidence rather than authority, and the courage to face results that may be negative or unwelcome. If he teaches history, he is trying also to teach the dimension of consciousness that only the sense of continuity with the past can give, the absence of which makes society as senile as loss of memory does the individual. If he is teaching literature, he is trying also to teach the ability to be aware of one's imaginative social vision, and so to escape the prison of unconscious social conditioning. Whatever he is teaching, he is teaching some aspect of the freedom of man.

I have put so much emphasis on the social function of literature because, in my experience, it is very little understood. In an age when silliness, or, more politely, absurdity, is sometimes thought to be an attribute of genuine vision, it is not surprising to hear some people say that all teaching of literature is an "establishment's" effort to impose a fool's paradise of imaginary values on the rest of society. One may see this to be nonsense and still not be able to formulate a social role for literature beyond the orbit of refined leisure-class amusement. But even if we do recognize its social role, we know that the real answer to any question about why we teach it does not lie in its relevance, or its social byproducts. Some subjects, like car-driving again, are a means to an end; the arts and sciences are not. Studying them is a process which is its own end, and exists for its own sake. Its products are incidental, and the usefulness of those products does not represent the value of the process, which is something quite apart from them.

In literature there is much to admire, but the end of literary study is not admiration of something remote, but the recognition that it corresponds to something within ourselves. Admiration is thus succeeded by possession, as we make what we read part of our own vision, and understand something of its function in shaping that vision. So far, it is true that education has been for the sake of the student: one wants literature to be something he can appropriate, and its study a process of transferring its power of vision to him. It is often said that there is no disinterested learning process for its own sake; that every such process is conditioned by the society it is in. Hence all scholarship is in a sense political: if it claims to be disinterested, it is really only defending the status quo. This is another way of saying that all our beliefs and actions take shape around a social vision constructed by the imagination. The important thing is to realize that no social vision is ever definitive; there is always more outside it. The circle of stories (or ocean of story, as it is called in India) is there to keep us continually expanding and reshaping that vision. It exists for us; it exists for itself; perhaps we may even feel, for a few moments in our lives, that it really is ourselves on an infinite plane.

Definitions

Ritual is a special human action maintaining rapport with the natural cycle.

Symbol is a unit of poetic meaning.

Myth unites ritual and symbol, giving action to thought and meaning to action.

Mythology is a set of myths that take root in a particular society. The most fully developed mythologies form an imaginative encyclopedia providing answers to questions of the deepest concern to society.

The *narrative patterns* of literature represent the absorption of ritual action into literature.

The symbols of literature recurring in different works of literature are called *archetypes.*

Literature shows various degrees of *displacement* of myths in the direction of the plausible, the moral or the "real."

Literature is the total body of stories and symbols that provides hypotheses or models of human behavior and experience.

The central story of all literature is the loss and regaining of *identity.*

A Structure for a Curriculum in Literature for the Secondary School

	Level 12	Level 11
CONCEPTS	Man's vision sees each individual as of supreme moral worth.	Man's revelations span the course o human wonder a wish.
OPERATIONS	The tragic action presents a hero in bondage isolated from his society.	The world of romance presents th dream of the her quest in which cha acters are stylized as heroic or villainous.
	The comic action presents a hero incorporated into a new society.	The world of iron and satire presents the nightmare of unfulfilled desire and frustrated effo

Level 10

Man's myths celebrate man's growth, decline, and rebirth.

Stories of the gods allow man to cope with the unknown and reduce his terror.

The quests of godlike heroes reflect man's search for his own identity.

Epic literature reflects society's vision of itself and its hope for the future.

Level 9

Man's oral and written traditions probe his origins and destinies.

The innocence of the garden, the wilderness of the desert, and the quest for another Eden provide the archetypes of romance.

The founding of the earthly city and its failure as an ideal provide the archetypes of tragedy and irony.

The regaining of the ideal society and free individual provide the archetypes of comedy.

Level 8

Man creates stories that unite his life with seasons.

The central story of literature begins in an innocent world and proceeds to the fallen world of experience.

The central story of literature ends with a rebirth of innocence and identity out of chaos and desolation.

Level 7

Man creates images that express his desires.

Literature humanizes the physical environment of man by contrasting the ideal world that ought to be with the real world that is.

A 2
B 3
C 4
D 5
E 6
F 7
G 8
H 9
I 0
J 1